This book is dedicated to:

Paris

Faith

Summer

&

All The Little Brown
Girls!

Little brown
girl,

your existence
alone,

makes it a
better world!

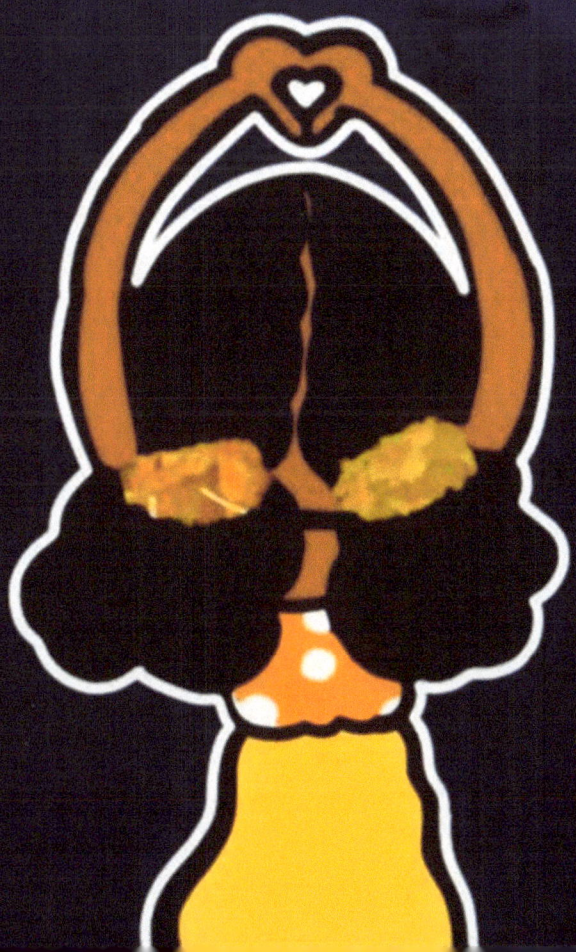

You mean what you say,
and say what you mean.

Strength of a warrior,
soft as a queen!

Eyes that sparkle,
like stars in the galaxy,

Hair growing upwards,

like nature's leaves,
defying gravity!

You weather the storm,
like a sunflower.

Rooted in faith,
and sure of the sun.

That's your
superpower!

Radiant skin,
kissed by the sun.

Serving bare-face,
you eat,

and leave no crumbs!

Turning darkness into light,
is your favorite trick,

changing the world,
a sprinkle at a time,

with your
black girl magic!

Special thank you to:

Mo'Nique
&
Sarah Jakes Roberts

Love,
The Little Brown Girls

AFFIRMATIONS

Everything
I Am,
Is More Than
Enough!

Don't let society's

standards,

control

YOUR standards,

endurance,

& capacity

-Keysha Roscoe

I am the writer
to my own
story!

www.ingramcontent.com/pod-product-compliance
Lightning Source LLC
Chambersburg PA
CBHW042020090426
42811CB00015B/1696